Slugs

Ashley Lee

Explore other books at:
WWW.ENGAGEBOOKS.COM

VANCOUVER, B.C.

e↱ WWW.ENGAGEBOOKS.COM

Slugs: Level 1
Backyard Bugs & Creepy Crawlies
Lee, Ashley 1995 –
Text © 2022 Engage Books
Design © 2022 Engage Books

Edited by: A.R. Roumanis

Text set in Epilogue

FIRST EDITION / FIRST PRINTING

LIBRARY AND ARCHIVES CANADA CATALOGUING IN PUBLICATION

Title: Slugs / Ashley Lee.
Names: Lee, Ashley, author.
Description: Series statement: Backyard bugs & creepy-crawlies
Engaging readers: level 1, beginner.

Identifiers: Canadiana (print) 20250448542 | Canadiana (ebook) 20250448569
ISBN 978-1-77878-710-2 (hardcover)
ISBN 978-1-77878-719-5 (softcover)

Subjects:
LCSH: Slugs—Juvenile literature.

Classification: LCC QL737.P94 C38 2025 | DDC J599.885—DC23

This project has been made possible in part
by the Government of Canada.

Canada

Contents

What Are Slugs?

Slugs are **mollusks**. They are related to clams and oysters.

Key Word

Mollusks: animals with soft bodies.

4

They are like snails without a shell. They do not have any bones.

What Do Slugs Look Like?

Slugs come in lots of colors. They can be gray, red, or blue.

Slugs have a hole in their side. This hole helps them breathe.

Slugs have about 27,000 teeth. That is more teeth than a shark!

Slugs have two **tentacles** that they can hide inside their heads. They help slugs see light.

Key Word

Tentacles: long, moveable limbs.

Where Do Slugs Live?

Slugs can be found all around the world. They do not live in very hot or very cold places.

Slugs live in places that are cool and wet. They mostly live in the ground.

What Do Slugs Eat?

Different kinds of slugs eat different things. A lot of slugs eat plants.

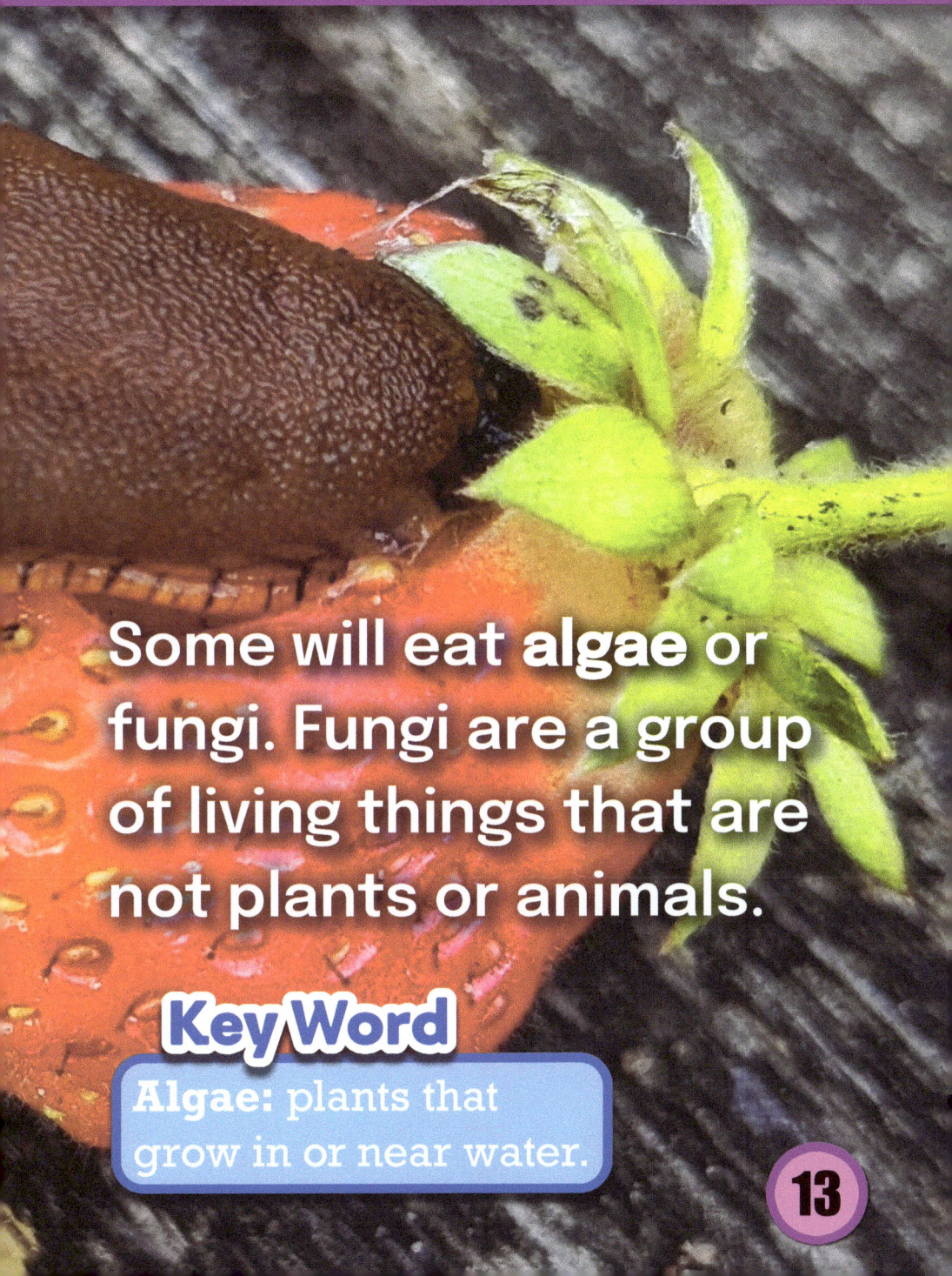

Some will eat **algae** or fungi. Fungi are a group of living things that are not plants or animals.

Key Word

Algae: plants that grow in or near water.

13

Some slugs eat other small animals. They will eat centipedes, worms, or bugs.

Some slugs will even eat other slugs. Many slugs eat whatever they can find.

Slug Behavior

Slugs make a slime called mucus. This helps them stay wet. Mucus also helps slugs crawl.

Slugs leave a trail of mucus behind them. It can help them find their way back to where they came from.

Slugs are often more active at night. They spend most of the night eating or looking for food.

Slugs sometimes come out when it rains. They may also come out on cold, cloudy days.

Slug Life Cycle

Slugs can lay about 40 eggs at a time. They often lay them in the soil or under rocks and leaves.

Baby slugs are called neonates. Some are as small as a grain of rice.

Neonates often stay close to home. They mostly eat algae and fungi.

Most slugs live for about a year. Some can live for five years.

Fun Facts

All slugs are both male and female.

Slug mucus is hard to wash off of skin.

Slug blood
is blue.

Some slugs
live underwater.

Are Slugs Helpful or Harmful?

Slugs are both helpful and harmful. Slugs help keep Earth clean by eating dead plants. Their poop keeps soil healthy.

Slugs often eat gardens filled with food for people. They can be hard to get rid of.

Are Slugs in Danger?

Many slugs are not in danger. But a few kinds are in danger.

Some slugs are losing their homes. People destroy the places they live.

Quiz

Test your knowledge of slugs by answering the following questions. The questions are based on what you have read in this book. The answers are listed on the bottom of the next page.

1 Do slugs have bones?

2 Do slugs mostly live in the ground?

3 Does mucus help slugs crawl?

4 Are slugs more active at night?

5 Are slugs both male and female?

6 Can slugs be hard to get rid of?

Explore other books in the
Backyard Bugs & Creepy Crawlies series!

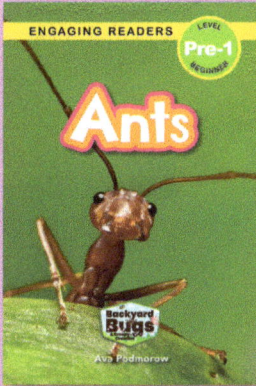

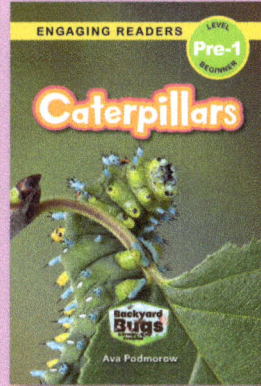

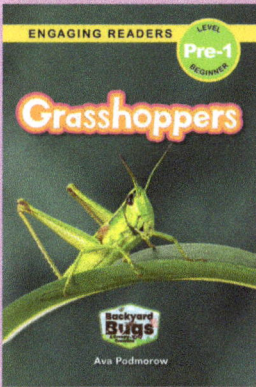

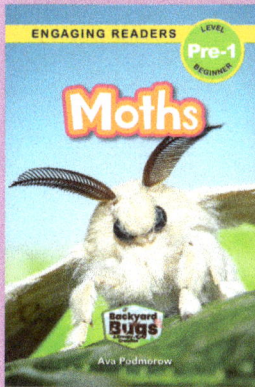

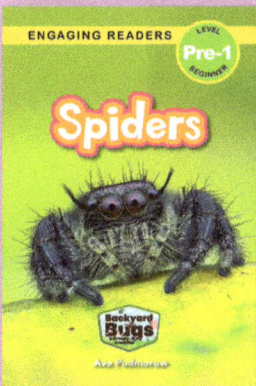

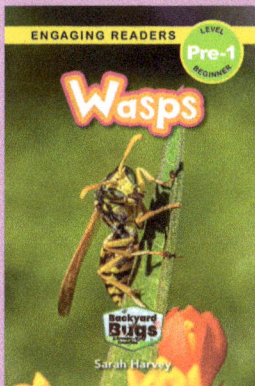

Visit www.engagebooks.com to explore more Engaging Readers.

www.ingramcontent.com/pod-product-compliance
Lightning Source LLC
Chambersburg PA
CBHW052037030426
42337CB00027B/5036